Along a
ROCKY SHORE

At low tide, a boy discovers tiny animals on a rocky seashore.

by Judith E. Rinard

**NATIONAL
GEOGRAPHIC
SOCIETY**

Washington, D.C.

Waves roll in and crash
against a rocky seashore.
In stormy weather, the
lighthouse warns ships
of the dangerous rocks.
A powerful light shines
in the round tower.

Here, the air smells fresh
and salty. Birds like the
gannet glide overhead,
looking for food. Many
small animals live on the
rocks, pounded by waves.
Can you guess where
they are hiding?

3

Twice each day, the sea rises and falls along the shore.
This movement is called the tide. There is more for you to see
if you explore when the tide is low. At high tide,
water covers much of the shore.

When the tide goes out, it leaves pools of water among the rocks. The tide pools are full of living things. Some hide there from the hot, drying sun or from hungry birds. A lobster has a hard shell that helps protect it. A spiny sun star crawls over a sea urchin to eat it.

NORTHERN LOBSTER, UP TO 36 INCHES LONG

SPINY SUN STAR, ABOUT 14 INCHES ACROSS

Look closely in tide pools and under rocks
and slippery seaweed. There, many animals
stay moist when the tide is out.

If you gently pick up a sea star, you can see
tiny tube feet on the underside of its arms.
Tube feet help it hold on to rocks when hit
by the waves. Fastened to rocks by sticky
threads, mussels stay safe inside hard shells.

HERMIT CRAB, ABOUT 2½ INCHES LONG, IN WAVY TOP SHELL

Tide pool animals must protect themselves to keep from being eaten. A hermit crab has no hard shell of its own. It moves into a shell left by another animal. An anemone is an animal that looks like a flower. The swimming anemone slips away to escape a sea star.

LEATHER STAR, ABOUT 15 INCHES ACROSS

SWIMMING ANEMONE (anem-o-nē), ABOUT 5 INCHES HIGH

11

GIANT PACIFIC OCTOPUS (BODY PLUS LONGEST ARM), ABOUT 16 FEET

HERMISSENDA NUDIBRANCH, ABOUT 3¼ INCHES LONG, AND TAYLOR'S COLONIAL TUNICATES, ABOUT 1/4 INCH HIGH

VERMILION ROCKFISH, UP TO 36 INCHES LONG

Long arms with suckers
help a giant octopus grab
and eat a shark. A sea slug
crawls over tiny animals
called sea squirts.
The sea slug is like
a snail without a shell.
A rockfish rests quietly.

Many birds find food along a rocky shore. A bald eagle swoops down and catches a fish with its claws. A sea gull nibbles on a sea star. Under the water, another sea star eats a mussel. Suction cups at the tips of its many little tube feet pull open the two parts of the mussel shell.

OCHRE SEA STAR, UP TO 20 INCHES ACROSS

Some birds, such as kittiwakes, build nests on cliffs high above the shore. They live in large groups called colonies, and they nearly fill the sky when they all take off at once. They dive into the sea to catch fish for their young. Showing off their colors, three puffins come face-to-face on an island near Alaska.

If you are lucky, you may see whales off some rocky shores. A humpback whale gulps a mouthful of water filled with fish as sea gulls circle above, hoping to catch some fish, too.

The whale strains fish out of the water with its baleen, the stiff bristles on its jaw. It pushes the water out of its mouth through the baleen. Then the whale swallows the fish trapped in the baleen.

You might see whales leap out of the water and fall back with a splash, as these two humpbacks are doing. This is called breaching. Nobody knows why whales breach, but some experts think they may often do this just for fun!

In summer, some large baleen whales catch little sea creatures called krill in cold northern waters. They travel south in winter to warmer waters.

Giant seaweed called kelp grows along California's rocky shore. Many animals, like garibaldi fish, hide in the waving underwater forest of kelp. Graceful sea lions swim nearby.

The kelp forest is also
the home of sea otters.
A mother sea otter
floats on her back,
holding her pup
on her chest.
These furry mammals
often relax and even
sleep this way.

When a sea otter is
hungry, it dives down
for a tasty snack—
a spiny sea urchin!
Sea otters love to eat
this prickly food.
Would you?

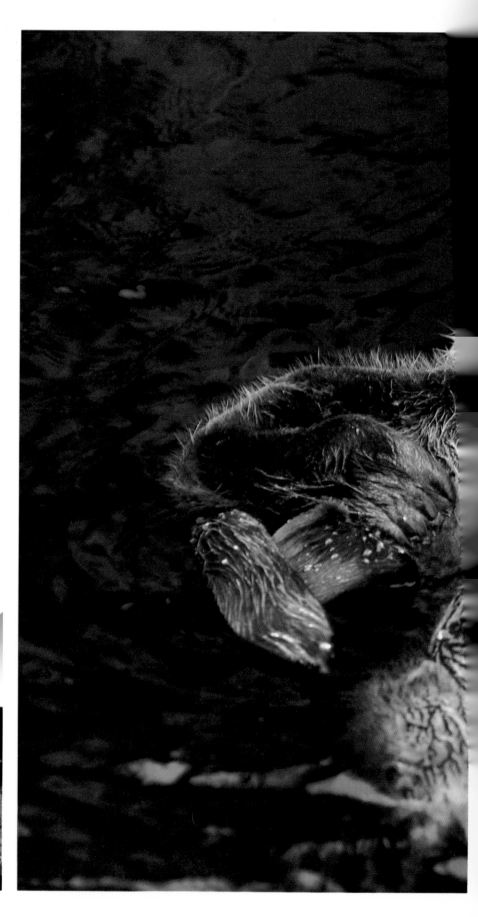

RED SEA URCHIN, ABOUT 5 INCHES ACROSS

Along northern rocky shores, herds of sea lions and walruses often climb up on rocks to rest and to warm themselves in the sun. A walrus can use its tusks, which are long teeth, to pull itself onto floating sea ice. Tusks also help a walrus fight off enemies.

Foaming waves smash along steep California cliffs. Protected by rocks, a sea lion finds a quiet spot to rest.

Wherever you go along a rocky shore, you can find animals at home. They live where waves crash and where water comes and goes with the tide.

More About Along a Rocky Shore

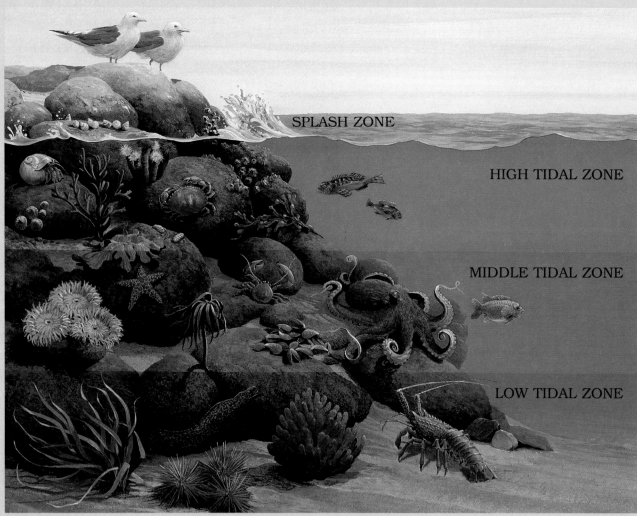

SPLASH ZONE

HIGH TIDAL ZONE

MIDDLE TIDAL ZONE

LOW TIDAL ZONE

LLOYD K. TOWNSEND

Like a tall building, a rocky seashore has many living levels, or tidal zones. Each is covered by water for different periods of time as the tides rise and fall. This painting shows animals and plants in all the zones. To identify them, match the names and numbers in the drawing on the next page.

Rocky seashores, where the waves pound and slam against coastal rock, are among earth's most dramatic regions. A seashore is an ever-changing environment that is governed by the pulsing rhythm of the tides. Twice a day, the tide surges in and covers the shore. Then it rushes out, leaving the rocks exposed to hot sun, pelting rain, and drying winds. In spite of these difficult conditions, a profusion of animals and plants competes for space on rocky coastlines.

A rocky shore can be divided into zones that vary according to how long they are covered by water as the tides rise and fall. The highest is the splash zone. It receives only ocean spray or storm waves. The second is the high tidal zone, which is dry except during the highest tides. The middle tidal zone is covered and uncovered by seawater twice a day. And the low tidal zone is always underwater except during the lowest tides.

The plants and animals living in each zone are remarkably well adapted to the harsh conditions there. All rocky shore creatures must withstand the continual battering of the surf. Many animals reduce the impact by hiding under seaweed or rocks or in crevices. Animals such as snails and crabs wear hard, armorlike shells.

To avoid being swept away by the waves, many creatures have ways of clinging to the rocks. Snails have a muscular foot that they use for moving slowly over the rocks or for holding fast in one place. Barnacles (1)* cement themselves to the rocks with a substance from their bodies. Mussels (1, 9) attach themselves with sticky byssus threads. Sea stars (8-11, 15) have rows of tiny tube feet with suction cups at the tips. These feet help the sea stars move around as well as cling tightly to rocks even in violent storms.

Some seaweeds (6-7, 9, 22-23) anchor themselves to the rocks with strong bases called hold-fasts. Seaweeds are slippery to walk on when they are exposed at low tide because they have a jellylike coating. It helps them hold in moisture and avoid drying out in the sun and wind.

The holdfasts and fronds of seaweeds provide food and moist shelter for many animals, especially those without protective shells, such as nudibranchs, also called sea slugs (13). Nudibranchs have rows of appendages that function as gills. Some may contain stinging cells that help protect the naked snail from enemies.

Many animals are frequent visitors to the rocky shore. Seals and sea lions (23, 26-27, 29, 32) come ashore to rest and have their young. Whales (18-21) feed on abundant fish and plankton off northern shores.

A good time to visit a rocky seashore is at low tide. Be sure you know the tide schedules. The tide can rise quickly. When you explore, wear shoes with non-slip soles. Look for tide pools, and observe the animals there. Try to see how they catch food. If you lift up seaweed or rocks, be sure to put them back so that the animals living underneath won't dry out. Do not take animals or plants away from their homes. Enjoy the shore, but protect it and its creatures.

*Numbers in parentheses refer to pages in *Along a Rocky Shore*.

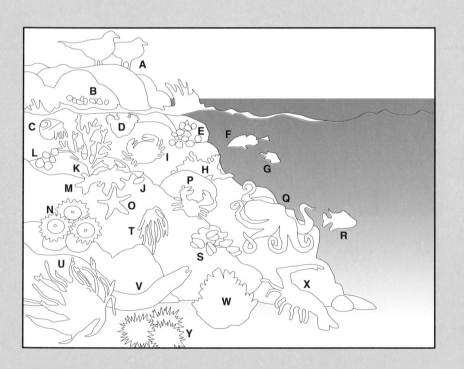

This drawing provides a key to the painting on the previous page: **(A)** *herring gull;* **(B)** *periwinkles;* **(C)** *hermit crab;* **(D)** *feather duster;* **(E)** *barnacles;* **(F)** *tide pool sculpin;* **(G)** *opaleye;* **(H)** *common rockweed;* **(I)** *rock crab;* **(J)** *chitons;* **(K)** *codium sponge seaweed;* **(L)** *limpets;* **(M)** *sea lettuce;* **(N)** *sea anemones;* **(O)** *sea star;* **(P)** *porcelain crab;* **(Q)** *octopus;* **(R)** *garibaldi fish;* **(S)** *mussels;* **(T)** *sea palm;* **(U)** *eelgrass;* **(V)** *moray eel;* **(W)** *red-beard sponge;* **(X)** *spiny lobster;* **(Y)** *red sea urchins.*

The text by Judith E. Rinard was prepared with input from scientific consultant Craig Phillips. Educational consultant Peter L. Munroe and reading consultant Dr. Lynda Bush also provided helpful comments and suggestions. Original research was provided by Alice Jablonsky. Prior to paperback publication, the National Geographic Society reviewed the book to ensure its accuracy in light of current information and study.

The photographs were selected by the National Geographic Society's illustrations editor Thomas B. Powell III.

CREDITS: Fred Bruemmer (cover); ENTHEOS (1, 4-5); Murray & Assoc., Inc./THE STOCK MARKET (2-3); Tom Brakefield (3); © Pat O'Hara (6); Fred Bavendam (7 lower, 11 both, 12-13, 13 upper); Breck P. Kent (7 upper, 8); © Ernest Braun (9); Thomas Cowell (10-11); Howard Hall (13 lower, 22-23); © Tom & Pat Leeson (14-15); Jeff Foott (15 upper); Joy Spurr/BRUCE COLEMAN INC. (15 lower); Steve Kaufman (16); Jeff Foott/DRK PHOTO (17); François Gohier (18-19, 20-21); Tom Bean (20); Stephen Frink/WATERHOUSE (23); Jett Britnell/DRK PHOTO (24); Frans Lanting/MINDEN PICTURES (24-25); © Boyd Norton (26); Stephen J. Krasemann/DRK PHOTO (27); Larry Ulrich/DRK PHOTO (28-29); Tom Mangelsen (29); Leonard Lee Rue III (32).

Library of Congress ⊆P Data
Rinard, Judith E.
    Along a rocky shore / by Judith E. Rinard.

        p. cm. — (Books for young explorers)
    Includes bibliographical references.
    ISBN 0-87044-822-6. (regular edition) — ISBN 0-87044-823-4 (library edition)
    Kids Want to Know paperback printing ISBN 0-7922-3611-4
    1. Seashore biology — Juvenile literature.   I. Title.   II. Series.
QH95.7.R56   1990
591.909'46—dc20   90-5583
                                                                    ⊆P

Visit our Web site at http://www.nationalgeographic.com or GO NATIONAL GEOGRAPHIC on CompuServe.

Balanced on a rock, a harbor seal enjoys a sunbath.

COVER: A sea lion looks out at the ocean from its home on a rocky island off the coast of Alaska.